Poster Sessions

A Guide to their Use at Meetings and Conferences for Presenters and Organizers

Alan Singleton

Published by
Elsevier International Bulletins,
Mayfield House, 256 Banbury Road, Oxford OX2 7DH, England

© British Library Board 1984

ISBN 0 946395 12 8
ISSN 0142-7288

Alan Singleton

Alan Singleton has worked in various aspects of the information and publishing industries for the past 13 years, including 5 as Research Fellow at the PCRC at the University of Leicester, during which he carried out research into scientific conferences and poster sessions. He is currently the European Manager of Scribe Publisher Services, a Faxon company.

Distributed in the Western Hemisphere by
ISI Press
3501 Market Street
Philadelphia PA 19104
USA

 British Library Cataloguing in Publication Data

```
Singleton, Alan
    Poster sessions : a guide to their use at
meetings and conferences - for presenters and
organizers.
    1. Meetings    2. Posters
    I. Title
    658.4'563    HF5549.5.C6

    ISBN 0-946395-12-8
```

CONTENTS

POSTER SESSIONS

PREFACE

This booklet aims to provide a guide to poster sessions: what they are, how and when to use them, practical dos and don'ts, help on poster design, and some advice on where to get materials.

Since about 1970, poster sessions have played an increasing role at scientific conferences and meetings. Their development has been most marked at the large international gatherings, although smaller meetings have also used them successfully.

Successful poster sessions come in all shapes and sizes, and with varying degrees of sophistication. We do not attempt to prescribe an 'ideal' poster session but rather to draw together those points which organizers and presenters need to consider.

ACKNOWLEDGMENTS

I would like to thank Louis Cohen and Doig Simmonds for useful comments on the text and Joyce Collins, Angela Chorley and Clarence Rickards for help with gathering material and text preparation. Thanks also to Trans World Congress Organisers for photographs and to all those university and other conference organisers who responded to my questionaire.

INTRODUCTION

What are poster sessions?

A poster session can take several forms, but essentially it is a means of allowing simultaneous 'presentation' and discussion of a variety of different pieces of research, normally at a conventional conference. A number of 'presenters' (usually more than ten, and sometimes as many as several hundred) displays his or her work at some sort of stand. The audience, or 'visitors', are free to wander round the displays, and engage the presenters in individual or group discussion. A typical session might last one and a half to two hours.

The poster session may have its origins in the traditional exhibition or *conversazione*, but there are some important differences: normally no equipment is displayed, and the presenters are researchers presenting research results, not sales or technical staff hoping to sell equipment or services.

How are they used now?

There is tremendous variety in the types of session currently held - variety in the style and size of posters, the length of the session, the place of presentation, the place in an overall conference programme, the type of information to be presented, the procedures for selection of the work to be presented, and the requirements made of presenters.

Normally poster sessions are held as *part* of an event. They are usually designed on the assumption that each visitor will be interested in only a few of the displays. Visitors are given sufficient time to make their selection and engage presenters in discussion. The overcrowding of conventional conference schedules is thus avoided. Although poster sessions are normally held as part of a larger conference, there is no reason why they should not be held alone, as indeed they have been on a few occasions - one recent international biomedical conference had all 1800 contributions in the form of posters.

The great majority of 'papers' given at poster sessions are 'contributed' or 'free' papers: they are submitted in response to a general invitation to contribute, rather than being specifically invited by the organizers. Thus they often correspond to the ten to fifteen minute presentations by researchers at traditional conferences. Invited papers are normally longer - perhaps given by an authority in the field - and often *review* a topic. An invited paper is therefore likely to be of interest to a substantial proportion of the audience, and less suited to poster form. Poster sessions are, in consequence, usually used for those papers which have interest to relatively small specialist groups.

So far poster sessions have found their main application in the sciences - medical and biomedical sciences especially. They are also widely used in other areas of the life sciences, as well as in chemistry and physics but are still relatively rare in the social sciences, humanities and, somewhat surprisingly, engineering. One would have thought that the display techniques of posters - pictures of equipment, graphs, etc - would have been well suited to engineering research.

Just to give an idea of the range, here are a few of the meetings which have used or plan to use poster sessions:

Title	Venue	Date
Biointeractions '84	London	January '84
International Savanna Symposium	Brisbane	May '84
12th Congress of the International Association for Bridge and Structural Engineering	Vancouver	September '84
Fifth International Conference on Titanium	Munich	September '84
Computers in Communication and Control	Brighton, UK	September '84
X World Congress of Cardiology	Washington DC	September '84

1 THE PROS AND CONS OF POSTER SESSIONS

Pros

1.   *A large number of 'papers' can be presented in a short space of time.* Parallel conventional sessions requiring delegates to choose between papers of potential interest can be avoided. So can the boredom of listening to several uninteresting papers while waiting for one or two of interest.

Poster sessions may also allow more time at the conventional sessions for invited or long papers of interest to all participants.

2.   *Informality.* Potentially, poster sessions allow more 'interpersonal' communication. For instance, an inexperienced researcher may benefit more from a critical opinion when he or she is not exposed to full public debate (as at a plenary session). Likewise, the visitor to the poster may find it easier to be frank when expressing criticism or ignorance.

As informality is a constructive feature of poster sessions, thought should be given to how to encourage it. One learned society has even recommended that investment in a supply of beer is money well spent (although see also point 4 below).

3.   *Ideally, individual participants, not presenters, choose which papers' (posters) to attend, and for how long.* A participant can assess interest from the programme, or by scanning the actual poster display. If well organized, displays will be posted before the session, and stay up afterwards, thus allowing browsing and extended note-taking during coffee or lunch breaks.

4.   *Flexibility in place of presentation.* Poster sessions can be set up in places unsuitable for conventional presentation such as interconnecting rooms, corridors or rooms with columns, low ceilings, poor acoustics, etc. They can also be set up near a conventional exhibition and be used to attract people to the exhibition. But it is important that poster sessions have some time when they are not in competition with alternative attractions (especially the bar).

5.   *Some types of material are particularly suitable for presentation in poster form.* Complex graphs and charts are rarely intelligible when presented on slides at conventional sessions, but can be readily accommodated at poster

sessions, as can any illustrations requiring more detailed study. In crystallography, for example, poster sessions are useful for presenting the results of crystal structure determinations where much of the detail is pictorial.

Cons

There are some disadvantages to poster sessions. But this is a guide to the use of poster sessions, so we suggest how good organizations can overcome some of these problems.

1. *A poster may seem to be of inferior status to a conventional paper.* This can be a real obstacle to successful poster sessions, and it derives in part from the policies of organizers. If, for example, organizers use poster sessions as dumping grounds for papers which are not quite good enough for 'proper' conventional publication, or *solely* for post-deadline papers, then clearly authors will also regard them in that light. Indeed, that seems to have happened in some cases in the medical field. Nevertheless, poster sessions may have a legitimate role to play even in such cases.

Papers should be chosen for poster presentation because that is the best method of presenting a particular piece of work on a given occasion. When examining a paper or potential poster, organizers should not confuse narrow interest in terms of *subject* matter, with limited interest in terms of *quality*.

There are a number of ways in which organizers can avoid giving posters 'inferior' status:

(i)   At some conferences *all* contributed papers are given as posters (with plenary conventional sessions reserved for the invited papers). This can be particularly appropriate if the invited papers are linked to the poster sessions, eg invited papers may review a particular speciality, and the next poster sessions show the latest work in that speciality.

(ii)   Contributed papers can be accepted or rejected for a conference *before* deciding on their mode of presentation. Organizers may later have to show some ingenuity to achieve a balance between conventional and poster sessions. But the potential flexibility of poster sessions should help. This still leaves the problem of *authors* who regard acceptance for poster presentation as second-rate. Thus the policy of the organizers must be made clear on the first announcement of the conference, and on any 'call for papers'.

(iii) Some organizers treat *all* contributions (poster and conventional) alike for publication of proceedings. For example, abstracts of *all* contributions may be produced before, or at, the conference, and presenters of posters may be required to produce a paper for publication. Their task is then similar to that facing the presenter at a conventional session, who may also have to write a paper for publication which is not just the typed version of the spoken paper.

(iv) Some organizers have tried the "positive discrimination" approach. They make sure that some of the best papers are presented as posters.

2. *Presenters at a poster session may not have the opportunity to see other displays at the same session.* Organizers can help by ensuring that posters are 'up' longer than the period of the session. At a large physics meeting in the USA, one third of presenters were asked to be at their stations for at least one hour of a three hour session. There was then sufficient time for all of them to get around.

Precisely how much time to set aside for presenters' viewing, however, depends on the number of posters at the session and the amount of information each poster, on average, communicates. Some poster sessions allow each presenter a 'booth' where a considerable amount of information can be displayed (see section 3); others provide only a single 2ft × 4ft board. In allocating presenters viewing time, organisers also have to consider the length of the session, the number of presenters and the space each is given - factors which are often dependent on subject matter.

Several authors presenting the same poster can, of course, take turns at attending their display. If a stand *has* to be left, it is a good idea to provide note-pads for visitors to leave messages.

3. *Popular displays may become over-crowded.* Over-crowding is more likely when a very small poster session (say 10-15 posters) is held at a large conference (more than 200 participants). However, it should then be possible to arrange for the small number of posters to be displayed throughout the conference. If a particular poster is continually crowded, then the item should have been given as a conventional paper - or the presenters are doing something they shouldn't!

3(a)   *Over-crowding around a popular poster can hinder access to an adjacent poster.* This problem should be considered when planning the session. Much can be done to avoid it by careful choice of poster equipment (which varies considerably in design) (see Section 3). Where time and space permits, alternate posters can be presented at different sessions (eg odd-numbered posters at one session, even numbered posters at the next).

4.   *Some material or topics will not be suitable for poster presentation.* We have already mentioned that review papers or those of very wide general interest are probably not suitable for posters. Neither are papers that mainly need detailed oral exposition. But posters, in fact, are rarely at a disadvantage compared with most 10-15 minute conventional oral presentations. Good visual aids, for example, are useful in both context; detailed material taking some time to assimilate seems better suited to posters; and computer print-out is unsuitable for both formats (unless it is enlarged in which case it might be acceptable in a poster).

5.   *Young researchers who present posters lose the 'tutorial' experience of presenting their topic to a large audience.* To what is extent this is a real loss is unknown. But, it may well be compensation to have the supposed advantages of direct communication with peers and more informal criticism.

2 DESIGN OF POSTERS

The design of a poster presentation will be constrained by a number of factors: eg the allotted surface area for each presentation, the money available, the facilities provided (such as lights, tables, etc) and the subject of the presentation. However, there are some simple hints which can help effective communication, whatever the resources or facilities.

General

The most general advice is quite obvious, but not always easy to follow; keep the presentation simple and clear, even if the topic is complex. The poster aims not only to inform, but also to attract interest. Titles and captions should be easy to read, and thus short (sub-titles can be added in the conference programme, if necessary, to preserve correct academic form). Prominent single word subheadings are more effective than the larger subheadings normally used in scientific papers.

Size of display

Not all organizers adequately inform presenters of the size and shape of display areas, even though they are major constraints on design. Knowing the size is an obvious requirement, but presenters also need to know the precise shape and orientation of the display area (eg long dimension vertical or horizontal, and rectangles side by side or one above the other). Thus, organizers should send presenters a dimensional sketch of the poster area.

The diagram shows a sketch of a poster layout similar to one actually used by an organizer. Note that it indicates a minimum distance between the lowest display item and the floor. It also indicates what authors should bring and what is provided. Some organizers, for example, prefer to provide authors with a card giving the title, number etc of their poster. In that case, the organizers should specify the size of the label on the diagram.

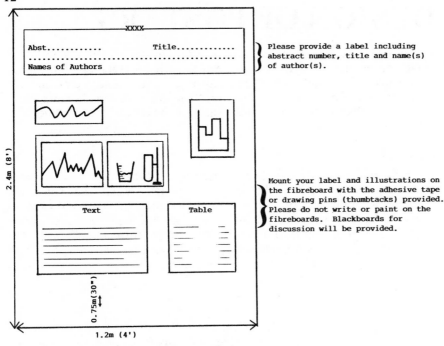

Please provide a label including abstract number, title and name(s) of author(s).

Mount your label and illustrations on the fibreboard with the adhesive tape or drawing pins (thumbtacks) provided. Please do not write or paint on the fibreboards. Blackboards for discussion will be provided.

Fig 1
Example of a typical poster layout
provided by an organiser

Text and graphics

The balance struck between text and graphics depends on the subject. But it is worth going to some lengths to include some graphics to break up the text. Graphics should be considered even when the subject does not easily lend itself to graphical treatment (remember that such a topic might well not be suitable for a poster session at all). Apart from the intrinsic interest of the subject of a presentation, the relative amount of detail given in text and graphics may well affect the amount of oral discussion that takes place ("Could you explain how this works?" "What is the object in the picture?" etc). At one poster session I attended, one presenter had covered his poster area (some 72 square feet in this case) with equations on general relativity. The display attracted some impressed glances, but relatively few discussants.

In considering the layout of text and graphics, there are two simple points which are important, but which are frequently over-looked.

(a)   Although the presenter knows his/her way around the poster, the viewer may not. Therefore the *sequence* of text and graphics must be clearly indicated, eg by using numbers, or arrows. (The viewer may have just come from a poster arranged entirely differently). Simple but prominent sub-headings like 'Introduction' and 'Conclusions' help.

(b)   Both organizers and presenters should ensure that there is somewhere for the presenter/s to stand or sit without obscuring the presentation - even if this requires less than maximum use of the poster boards.

Size of lettering

Obviously, the larger the lettering the more limited is the amount of information that can be displayed; the smaller the lettering, the nearer viewers have to approach to read it. If the presenter has a popular topic, crowds may gather around the poster. Clearly, if there is sufficient space in the poster room, large lettering would allow a less congested view. In such cases, large lettering should therefore be considered at the cost of reducing the amount of detail. There is evidence that capital letters in continuous text reduce the speed of reading (as compared with lower case letters of the same body size). However, capitals are more easily discernible at a distance. This suggests that capitals should be used in titles and short sub-headings, with lower case more suitable for general text on a poster.

Titles probably need to be seen easily at five metres or more and should thus be quite large, at least 20-30 mm in height. The rest of the text need not be as large. There are differences of opinion as to what is the best viewing distance - one opinion is that, since visitors will be discussing the poster with the presenter near to the poster (say within a metre), the main text need only be legible from within that distance. However, a more persuasive opinion is that posters are not only for discussants, but also for those who wish to view without, or before, entering discussion. Thus, in order to prevent unnecessary congestion, a size of lettering legible from 2.5-3 m (8-9 feet) would be most suitable.

Simmonds and Reynolds[1] have a useful rule of thumb for working out the appropriate letter size for different viewing distances.

$$\frac{\text{Distance from eyeball to lettering in metres}}{0.25} = \text{height of lettering in millimetres}$$

Table 1 uses this formula to give the relationship between letter size and maximum viewing distance for five different distances. (An alternative table giving smaller letter sizes is given in the Kemp and Corwell book, Planning and Producing Audiovisual Materials[2].)

Table 1: Relationship Between Maximum Viewing
Distance And Letter Size

Viewing distance	Minimum letter height
1 m (3.3 ft)	4 mm (0.16 in)
2.5 m (8.3 ft)	10 mm (0.4 in)
3.75 m (12.5 ft)	15 mm (0.6 in)
5 m (16.7 ft)	20 mm (0.8 in)
10 m (33.4 ft)	40 mm (1.6 in)

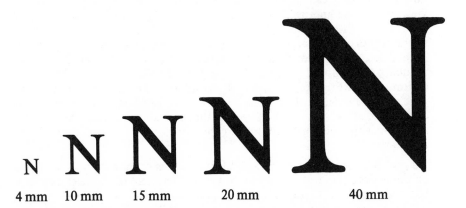

| 4 mm | 10 mm | 15 mm | 20 mm | 40 mm |

Clearly a presenter could use a variety of letter sizes, depending on the information to be conveyed and the target audience: eg largest size to inform the viewer what the presentation is about; intermediate size to give a quick overview; smaller sizes for more detail for the very interested viewer. Material, which is to be read generally, should be viewable from about 2.5 m and thus needs to be at least 6 mm (0.25 in) in size ie

N

Note that the size of the typeface used in this report is 10 pt, which is hardly suitable for a poster! (Standard typewriter size is 2.5 mm, which again is not suitable for poster presentation.)

Therefore, in summary, the minimum letter sizes to use are as follows:

titles: use # CAPS

(these are 20 mm to be viewable from 5 m)

subheadings: use ## CAPS

or ## lower case

(these are 12.5 mm to be viewable from 3 m)

general text: use mainly ## lower case

(these are 10 mm to be viewable from 2.5 m)

Lines in graphics should be at least 2 mm thick to be easily discernible at 2.5 m ie.:

The space between lines used for shading should be about four times the line thickness.

Production of lettering

There are many techniques for lettering, but a presenter may be limited by the technical facilities available. For titles and headings, dry transfer lettering (such as Letraset, Rapitype (much cheaper) or one of the other ten or so makes available) should suffice. Remember though that the transferred letters need spraying with an adhesive varnish to prevent peeling.

Dry transfer lettering must be done carefully, using guide lines to maintain line position. Misplaced letters can usually be removed by a small piece of masking or adhesive tape.

One alternative for titles and headings is stencil which can be cheaper than dry transfer lettering if the equipment is already available. It needs a little practice to be proficient, although even dry transfer lettering takes some time to master. Of course, an illustration department will be able to give advice, or perhaps loan equipment - assuming that the department is not carrying out the work.

There is a large variety of plastic stencils available. If you are doing the stencilling yourself, check that the stencil or the template has edges or levels which raise the openings of the stencil from the paper, so that ink will not flow under the plastic. Small areas of unwanted ink or lettering can be removed with a scalpel.

Spacing for both dry-transfer and stencilled lettering needs special care. It can be difficult to space capital letters so that the effect is pleasing. Equal spacing will not always be appropriate, because of the differing shapes of different letters. Fig 2 makes the point. In 2 i), the distance between letters is equal, but in 2 ii) the *area* between letters is roughly equal. 2 ii) looks the best. Incidentally, this illustration is taken from an excellent book on presentation of data[1], which has over 200 pages of advice on design and production techniques, for those who want to go into the topic in more detail.

Fig 2 (i)
The linear *space between the characters is equal, but the effect is uneven.*

Fig 2 (ii)
Here the area *of space between characters has been judged by eye to be approximately equal; the spacing now appears to be more even.*

(Figure courtesy of Martinus Nijhoff BV, Medical Division)

The greater the viewing distance, the greater should be the space between lines of lettering. As general rules: there should always be more space between lines than between words; the space must allow room for the ascenders and descenders of letters (eg the bottom of a 'y' must not touch or overlap the top of an 'h' the space between the bases of two lines should not be less than one and a half times the height of the capital letter of the face being used).

If other techniques are not available, text (as long as there is not too much of it) can be hand printed (if the organizers allow). However this obviously has to be done carefully. Letters should be somewhat (depending on the quality of writing!) larger for each viewing distance, than the numbers given in table 1.

Many presenters will have access to some 'audio-visual' department which may have a relatively unsophisticated 'headliner' or 'phototypesetter' capable of producing good quality letters for titles and headings.

If you work at an organization with a large computer it might be worth enquiring whether there are any computer graphics facilities which might be of use. For example, at the University of Leicester, the computer laboratory's Graphics Centre has recently introduced a 'Poster Program' which facilitates the computerized production of a mixture of text and graphics (in four colours), at sizes suitable for poster presentation.

General text

With even limited audio-visual facilities, ordinary text can be produced by photographic enlargement. For this, the use of electronic typewriters using carbon ribbon is preferred - the enlargement from a cloth ribbon will not usually give the required quality. Double-spaced typing is the easiest to read after enlargement, although some would say that single-spacing is adequate for detailed information for the specialist viewer.

The photographic method has a lot to recommend it, since it is relatively cheap and quick. If possible, use matt finish rather than glossy paper.

Type face

If there is a choice (as there will be for stencilling, dry-transfer lettering, or 'headlining'), simple typefaces without serifs should be used. (Serifs are the short cross lines at the ends of the main strokes, used in some typefaces.)

Ideally, the typeface of titles and text should match, but this is a less important consideration than that each should be simple and of a suitable size.

Graphics

Overall, the design of graphics for posters is similar to that for other media, and we will here mention only features peculiar to poster presentations.

One of the advantages of poster sessions is their ability to allow prolonged perusal of graphs, diagrams, etc. Nevertheless, the clearer and simpler the better. The type of illustration may well be determined by the subject matter, but even so there are some simple points which are worth bearing in mind.

If the graphics have been prepared for other purposes, they may need to be enlarged for poster presentation. For general viewing, lettering on graphics needs to be about 6 mm (quarter inch) high, and any lines no thinner than 2 mm. Drawings that are to be photographically enlarged should be done in black ink (or black tape), on a white background. Colour can be added afterwards - strips of coloured adhesive acetate film or tape will give a professional appearance.

Photographs

Ideally, photographs should have good contrast and sharp focus, and should not contain unnecessary or distracting detail. Where the size of the photographed object will not be apparent to an interested viewer, some indication of scale should be included (eg inclusion of a familiar - but not distracting - object in the photograph, or a line drawn to indicate scale). If a photograph is to be mounted onto a backing sheet, it is wise *not* to use a water-based glue, since this may well cause the photograph to wrinkle.

Each graphic and/or photograph should have its own clear caption or legend. The caption should be set horizontally.

Originals

It is risky to use the originals of graphics of photographs, especially if they are to be subsequently used for publication. In such a case, photographic copies should be obtained.

Having prepared the poster and layout, do not forget to label the text and graphics so that you, the presenter, know where each piece will go. This is probably best done by marking the back of each sheet in the centre (in case you later decide to trim an illustration, and thereby lose the edge). Some organizers give presenters only a short time to set up the display, and clear labelling helps to prevent panic!

The time it takes

The best advice is not to underestimate the time it takes to produce a good poster. Total poster areas vary from 8 to 72 square feet, so it is not easy to suggest what the average time would be for an 'average' quality poster. In one experimental poster session, however, presenters spent, on average, six to ten hours on preparation, although most of them felt that they should have spent more. Interestingly, these presenters unanimously felt that the preparation of a conventional paper would have taken up more of their time[3].

Mounting and transport

Depending on the type of facilities available to organizers and presenters, the 'pre-mounting' of text and graphics can be considered ie mounting the presentation on backing boards of a size that will fit in a briefcase, and then, at the poster session, mounting those boards on the poster board. (Cards of larger size may be scored on the back and folded). This can have a number of advantages: it protects the material, makes it easier to put up and take down the presentation and can add to a display's visual appeal (eg confronted backing boards should highlight text). However, it also has some disadvantages: it costs a little more; the allotted poster space may not coincide with the amount needed for the boards - and, similarly, less information can be displayed if backing boards are used. Ideally, organizers should say what type of poster board will be available. If they do not issue this information, then presenters who want to mount their display on boards should check with the organizer.

Summary

Here is an abbreviated 'check list' of points:

Lettering	— 'n' height of 10 mm should be viewable from 2.5 m - Titles 20 mm for 5 m viewing
	— dry transfer lettering needs spraying with adhesive varnish
	— photographic enlargement of typing should be printed with matt finish
Typeface	— should be simple, probably *sans serif*
Graphics	— should be simple if to be viewed at a distance, lines a minimum of 2 mm thick
	— use black ink
	— can use colour adhesive tape for caption or legend

Photographs	— should have good contrast and sharp focus
	— should give an indication of scale
	— do not affix with water-based glue
	— use a caption or legend
Overall	— ensure a balance between text and graphics; sequence to be labelled or arrowed or otherwise made clear
	— make sure sheets/cards, etc are labelled on the back so that *you* know where they go
	— do not obscure presentation by standing directly in front.

Organizers

We deal with organizing procedures later. Here we suggest what the organizers might tell the presenter about design. Each poster session is different, and will have its own constraints. We would urge that organizers clearly spell out the constraints operating, but make only the minimum *specifications* on poster design: for example, the organizers may want all titles of papers/posters, and authors'/presenters' names to be displayed in a uniform and specified way (they may even want to do it themselves).

However, organizers should avoid detailed *prescriptions* of how text and graphics are to be displayed. This is simply because the subject of each poster may require different treatment, and the preparation facilities available to presenters will probably vary considerably. Laying down precise prescriptions is therefore likely to hamper effective communication.

Nonetheless, organizers might like to suggest design details of the 'hints' variety, perhaps using this section as a guide. The one possible exception to this is where there is a detailed plan for 'publication' of the poster papers in hard copy form eg as part of a published proceedings. Presenters should, of course, have been informed prior to the session on matters relating solely to the publication such as copyright etc (see section 4). However, if publication will put strict requirements on such things as preparation of graphics, etc, then these should be communicated to presenters well in advance of poster presentation, so that the presenters can decide whether they are going to prepare original graphics differently for poster presentation. If laboriously prepared originals (which have been enlarged for poster presentation) do not meet the requirements for publication, through no fault of the presenters, justifiable frustration and much waste of time would result.

With respect to design, organizers should give presenters some general hints and guidelines, while also telling them:

a)   The size of their poster area, its configuration and orientation (see section 3).

b)   The type of poster board to be used and how material can be mounted.

c)   The range of additional facilities available (lights, chairs, etc).

d)   The location of space in which presenters can stand.

While assisting presenters in this way, some poster session organizers have offered a prize for the best designed poster, so as to stimulate good design. Such a prize need not be trivial: eg a subscription to an important journal, or a current awareness information service. I have not heard of any wooden spoons being given!

3 POSTER AREAS AND EQUIPMENT

Areas

In an earlier section we mentioned that poster sessions have the advantage that they can be held in a variety of different types of location: halls, rooms, laboratories, hallways - even, it has been suggested, in hotel lobbies. However, not all these are equivalent. The type of board most suitable will be different in different areas and the areas themselves have their own advantages and disadvantages.

Area	Points to note
Near the bar	Attracts participants near bar opening times, but may compete with bar; requires that poster sessions be timed accordingly.
Corridors, hallways	In the traffic flow and may therefore attract many passers-by. However, passers-by may continue to 'pass-by': consideration must be given to safety regulations.
Laboratory benches	Likely to be readily available in a university; probably limited display space so small boards required to fit benches. Allows equipment relevant to an accompanying poster display to be demonstrated.
Rooms	Rooms not appropriate for conventional presentation to a seated audience, may be suitable for poster sessions and may be relatively cheap to hire. However, rooms need to be located near to the other activities, especially if they are small.
Halls	Similar considerations as for rooms. May be useful if main meeting hall has ancillary hall.
With exhibition	May provide useful 'cross interest' ie participants going to the exhibition, also see the posters, and vice versa. Posters and exhibits *can* be intermixed or in separate sections.

Within any one area, certain positions will be more desirable. Posters near 'traffic' eg doorways, will probably attract attention; some positions will be well lit (eg those near windows), making it easier to see presentations.

Other points

(i) For some of the more unusual areas in particular (corridors, foyers, etc), someone will need to check that poster presentations will not be in breach of any safety regulations. Consideration will also have to be given to whether there are any safety implications not covered by the regulations (eg poster boards sufficiently stable, etc). In addition, insurance needs should be assessed, perhaps as part of conference needs as a whole.

(ii) *Status.* We have already discussed the status of poster presentations in relation to the prestige they convey on their presenters. Organizers anxious to preserve or improve that status should think carefully about the positioning of poster displays. Location in out-of-the-way or auxiliary places (eg mixed up with exhibitions of equipment) would diminish the presenter's potential kudos.

(iii) *Setting-up and Taking-down.* Posters will require certain periods in which to be assembled and dismantled. Clearly, in a crowded programme with several poster sessions, a lot of setting-up and taking-down of displays could cause chaos in hallways or other areas which are also main thoroughfares.

EQUIPMENT

Boards come in many shapes and sizes. Organizers may find that their planned venue already has facilities, and they will probably then have to tailor their plans accordingly. If not, boards can be hired from some learned institutions and from specialist commercial organizations, including those who specialise in exhibitions. Names and addresses of some of each source are given later in this section.

Boards and layouts are by no means unimportant. The following photographs show a couple of poster sessions, with annotations to point out some of the problems that can arise. Some such problems are probably unavoidable, since organisers will probably be faced with the constraints of limited funds, space, and availability of equipment. But some can be avoided.

(Photograph by courtesy of Trans World Congress Organisers)

Fig 3 *Free standing board. Many posters can be contained in a small area (using back and front of the board). Note that this particular arrangement is useful mainly for those listening to the discussion since presenter and discussant obscure half poster.*

(Photograph by courtesy of Trans World Congress Organisers)

Fig 4 Free standing board as in Fig 3. However, here only alternate boards are used in session, allowing room for presenter to stand, but less room for presentation. Note that there is no provision for the placing of presenter's files, papers, etc, with the inevitable result on the floor.

Note also that the titles and numbers of the boards are only a little above head height, and therefore may be difficult to locate.

Boards and benches

Another common type is the board for use on, say, a laboratory bench (see Figure 5).

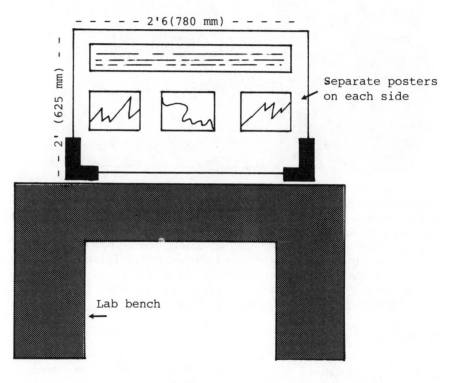

Fig 5
Board on laboratory bench

These are very simple and include a board held in place by a wooden frame. The whole is positioned in the centre of a laboratory bench and each side is used for a separate poster presentation. As can be seen, these boards are quite small and, we would suggest, constitute the *minimum* size required for an effective poster. With this type of presentation there should be room for one presenter to sit near the presentation. As one might expect, presenters

and discussants often sit *on* the lab benches themselves, which can obscure the poster. A further problem is that benches with unattended posters quite quickly get taken up by conference participants who happen to meet there and discuss matters totally unconnected with the poster. This is less likely to occur if the area of the bench in front of the poster is used for notepads, offprints, etc (if allowed). But that is only a minor deterrent - better for the poster to be attended, at least at specified 'sessions'.

Walls

Wall posters are not confined to China. A couple of organizations we have contacted mentioned that they have used walls for mounting poster sessions. The use of walls, however, may put constraints on the method of mounting (eg six inch nails will have to be prohibited!). Organisers will also have to decide whether posters are to be pre-mounted on boards and, if so, who is to provide the boards. Presenters will need to be notified accordingly.

Free-standing boards

As we have seen, free-standing boards come in a variety of sizes, and are obviously the most use in otherwise empty rooms, halls, etc. The Institute of Physics (IoP) uses, and has available for hire, basic board units 4 ft (1.2 m) wide × 3 ft (0.9 m) high. They are covered with hessian and are double-sided. Of course, the boards can be used in different configurations, but the IoP chooses at its meetings to construct booths 6 ft high using six boards, as shown in Figure 6.

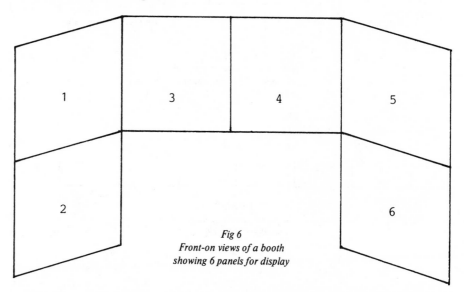

Fig 6
Front-on views of a booth
showing 6 panels for display

Such a booth is much larger than the arrangements shown in the photographs (Figures 3-4) and it has the advantage of providing sufficient room for presenter, chair, papers and a clear view by a number of visitors.

If we take a six-board booth, similar to that used by the IoP, we can easily illustrate different ways of arranging booths to fit into different shapes of hall. Figure 7 shows, in plan view, four different arrangements of six booths.

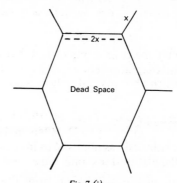

Fig 7 (i)
'Tower' or 'Drum' arrangement of
6 booths. (24 boards used)

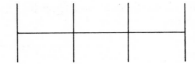

Fig 7 (ii)
'Herring bone' arrangement of
6 booths. (22 boards used)

Fig 7 (iii)
Simple linear arrangement of
6 booths. (26 boards used)

Fig 7 (iv)
Arrangement of 6 booths. (24 boards used)

The most efficient arrangement in terms of number of boards used is 7 ii). Almost as efficient is the adaptation shown in 7 iv). That arrangement would use only 20 boards if the end booths had only one board on each wing instead of two.

Figure 8 shows an arrangement used by the Federation of European Biochemical Societies for a meeting in Dresden in 1978. At this enormous conference all 1800 contributed (as opposed to invited) papers were given as posters in two main halls. Flat poster stands were used.

The arrangement in one of the halls taken from the conference booklet is shown. An exhibition was mounted on the perimeter of the central poster area so that participants could move easily from one to the other.

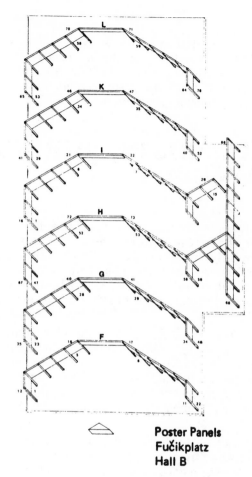

Poster Panels
Fučikplatz
Hall B

Fig 8
Arrangement of poster panels in one
of the halls used at the 12th Feb's
meeting (Dresden, July 1978)

Of course most poster sessions are much smaller than this - some have only a
dozen or so presentations. Nevertheless, whatever the scale it is important to
plant the arrangement of posters in order to minimize cost and maximize
effective communication. An organizer should therefore visit the meeting
site to determine rough dimensions of the poster area and the positioning of
entrances and exits. A diagram or model can then be drawn up to see what
can be accommodated, and in what configuration.

Setting up

Setting up poster boards/booths is a task which should not be underestimated. The 170 boards kept by the IoP need a 2-ton truck for their transport, and to set up 20-30 of the six board booths is likely to take three people, three hours or more. Some poster equipment manufacturers give set-up times in their equipment specifications.

GENERAL COSTS, HIRING AND PURCHASE

General costs

Here we are mainly concerned with costs of equipment. We should however comment on costs of poster sessions in general. Most costs associated with poster sessions are fairly straightforward, but 'visible' costs (ie actual money expended) will vary enormously, depending both on the size of the session and the amount of 'hidden' subsidy provided by a host institution eg, in hall or room hire, provision of poster boards, labour for setting up and dismantling, etc.

Savings may be achieved by not having to provide extra audio-visual services for conventional parallel sessions (projectors, screens, technicians), and by cheaper rental rates for halls/rooms not suitable for conventional oral presentations. On the other hand, extra expenses can be incurred if the organizers pay for the production of a title and a number to be attached to each poster. In addition, an organiser may decide to provide stationery, pins, pens, etc.

Certainly organisers should have such things as drawing pins, 'Blu-tack' etc, available for those who forget to bring, or are not aware that they should bring, their own. At least one conference has paid for 'poster assistants' to help presenters and delegates at the sessions.

Thus organisational costs are dependent on the wishes of the organisers and the policy of the host institution. Clearly they have to be assessed separately for individual cases.

Who can provide facilities

Some organisations do hire out poster equipment. For example, Table 2 gives details and daily hire charges for the panels available from the IoP. As an example, assume that the largest boards were hired for 24 booths, to be set up as in Figure 7 iv), giving roughly 72 sq ft of display area, ie requiring just under 100 boards, without shelves, etc. This would cost about £75 per day, at 1984 prices. An additional cost would be made for transport (from Stoke Poges) - within 40 miles this cost would be £40 to £50. So, if a fairly large conference is being held (say four days), with poster sessions on each day (say two separate sessions a day), then hire of 100 boards would mean that 192 papers could be presented in posters for a hire charge of something over £350 including transport, but without other costs like room hire etc.

TABLE 2: Poster session equipment available for hire from the Institute of Physics

Unit	Stock	Description	Daily hire charge per unit 1984
AOP	177	Framed softboard panel 955 × 1214 mm framed in steel, covered both sides in limestone hessian, total weight 6.73 kg.	85p
A1	54	As above except dimension 866 × 619 mm, total weight 3.66 kg.	45p
AOH	30	As above except dimensions 192 × 1214 mm, scarlet hessian, total weight 2.50 kg.	45p
SFC	83	Shelf, timber covered in black textured PVC 620 × 1189 mm with clips weight 6.25 kg.	65p
SCL	106	Ladder frame to support shelves 614 × 952 mm made of 7 mm diameter mild steel, bright chrome finish, weight 3.64 kg.	45p
S/W		110 × 1-way) Connector for 97 × 2-way) frames, aluminium 100 × 4-way) tube	gratis
S/W	228	Footpad, grey plastic with inset 4-way connector	gratis
S/TB		139 × 1-way) Top cap for frames, 127 × 2-way) grey plastic 47 × 4-way)	gratis

| SB | 25 | 4-way spider box with 13A plug and 10 metre cable. | 75p |

Other organizations also provide poster board equipment. For this booklet, we have undertaken some surveys to see how readily such equipment will be available. We contacted more than 50 universities and colleges, 30 large learned societies, and a number of local commercial organizations, listed in our local 'yellow pages' telephone directory under 'Exhibition stand contractors'.

These surveys produced some interesting results. On the one hand, it showed how important poster sessions are becoming at some venues. On the other, several specialist conference organisers were still unaware of them. Of 41 university and college responses, 22 (54%) had provided facilities for poster sessions. The implications if you are organising a poster session are clear. If the venue is already determined, the organisers of the session need to establish whether the hosts are familiar or experienced with poster sessions. If they are not, the organisers will probably have to make increased efforts to ensure a satisfactory session.

Universities and colleges

Our survey of universities and colleges consisted of sending out questionnaires to organizations listed in the 'Conference and Exhibitions Yearbook: London, York Publications, Annual', and other advertising material. We asked a number of questions on whether they could supply and erect the display boards, and whether they would hire out equipment to conferences taking place elsewhere.

Of our 22 respondents who had provided facilities for poster sessions, all but one could supply boards themselves. The odd one out would hire them. Only one institution providing its own boards said that it could not erect them. All institutions would provide suitable audio-visual equipment to accompany the poster session if requested.

Most institutions with their own boards, however, had not loaned them out to conferences taking place elsewhere. The exceptions were the universities at Aberdeen, Salford, Stirling and Warwick. Of those that had not loaned boards, only Durham University said that it would be willing to do so if asked.

The scale of charges and the method used to work them out were very varied. Charges for the hire of boards were in some cases worked out on a daily rate, in others on a weekly rate and in others were a flat rate for the duration of the conference. One respondent made no board charge.

Some institutions levied a labour charge for erecting boards etc. Others said simply that their charges were negotiable. And one respondent said that charges for poster sessions were normally free provided "the residential element of the conference is substantial".

Of the 19 respondents to our questionnaire who had not provided facilities for a poster session, 15 said that they would be willing to do so.

Learned societies

Learned societies are much less involved, it seems, in the direct provision of poster facilities, and only the IoP, among our respondents, will hire equipment to outside bodies. Sixteen of 30 large learned societies replied, five of which had furnished a poster session. Five (not entirely the same five) had offered some sort of guidance to organizers and presenters, which varied from a few lines of advice, to a page or so. Some of those societies that have their own conference premises will also have display boards available for conferences but, in the main, organizers are left to their own devices.

Commercial conference centres etc

A few years ago I contacted a number of commercial organizers of conferences and found that few had *heard* of poster sessions, let alone organised one. The picture has now changed somewhat. A number of organisations currently claim expertise in the organization of poster sessions, as well as the provision of boards. However, it appears that the most will only provide boards (etc) as part of an organizing package.

Some organizations are still not aware of poster sessions, but, in accordance with good commercial practice, remain confident - as one said: "I don't know what you mean by a poster session, but I expect we could cope with it". Below we list the commercial conference organizers who responded specifically on poster sessions and some of their responses.

Conference Organizer/Name	*Response*
Swan House Special Events Ltd Exhibition Organisers & Consultants Swan House Swan Road Hanworth, Middlesex TW13 6TP (Walton-on-Thames 243866)	For several years now been supplying posterboards to international congresses, national conferences . . . also undertake all aspects of the posterboard use - site survey, plan layouts, design & publication of the presentation material for the boards, transport & erection, and administration of the actual sessions

for which the boards are intended and layouts of the boards to the presenters. Charges: 1 quote on each application separately.

Conference Clearway
Conference House
9 Pavilion Parade
Brighton BN12 1RA
(0273-695811/694079)

Poster sessions are becoming increasingly popular and effective. We advise organising committees on the best venue, method or present-ation, most economical budget. Quote for specific cases.

Wembley Conference Centre London
Wembley
HA9 0DN
(01-902-8833)

Poster sessions are playing an increasingly important part in medical and scientific conferences, and naturally we can provide the organisers with any technical requirements that they might need . . . we do carry a cross section of equipment . . . most of these items are charged separately to our room fees and are normally charged on a per-item basis.

Brighton Civic Conference Venues
Brighton Resort Services Department
Marlborough House
54 Old Steine
Brighton BN1 1EQ
(0273-29801 Ext 8140)

A number of scientific and medical conferences held in the Brighton Centre since it opened in 1977 have been staged very successfully. We have the advantage of very large foyers where the posters can be set up without disturbing the conference sessions. We have various halls, all with a flat floor where poster sessions could be organised.

Barbican Ctr for Arts & Conferences
Barbican
London
EC2Y 8DS
(01-638-4141)

We have two areas in which poster sessions may take place . . . concourse and Exhibition Halls . . .
In the concourse area we are providing panels on 2 ft, 4 ft and 6 ft modules which can be hired direct from us . . . in the Exhibition Halls we have a shell scheme built into the halls . . . this is a plywood based

structure covered with a nylon loop fabric to which both posters or small exhibits can be attached by Velcro Dots. Both systems have lighting attachments.

St David's Hall
National Concert & Conference Hall of Wales
Cardiff CF1 28H
(0222-42611)

Given sufficient notice, it would be possible to arrange poster boards through other sources . . . we have a number of rooms as well as foyer spaces which could be used . . . each event negotiated individually.

National Exhibition Centre Ltd
Birmingham
B40 1NT
(021-780-4141)

We have all the facilities on hand to organise an event . . . for smaller meetings such as poster sessions we would recommend one of our Private Hospitality Suites. Rental charges . . . are negotiated between NEC and the individual organizer.

Our enquiries were sent to 19 conference centres and 12 conference organizers. Although several sent general brochures, the above represent the specific responses on poster sessions.

Buying your own equipment

Let us imagine that, as organizers of conferences, you have held several successful poster sessions using hired equipment, and are now considering purchasing your own boards, etc. The obvious piece of advice is to shop around, since there are several makes of board on the market.

You will be able to find suppliers of agents through your local telephone directory. We found no difficulty in getting a response locally.

In addition to straightforward suppliers or agents for a particular make, it may be well worthwhile going through a firm able to supply from a number of manufacturers, since it is then possible to benefit from their advice. One such firm is Photobition, whose address is given at the end of this section. Photobition's Fulham showroom displays equipment from several different manufacturers.

Advice may well be needed, and it will naturally be important that the customer has identified his or her needs as well as possible. For example, the following factors should be considered:

1. Money.

2. Space available for display.

3. Desired poster sizes.

4. Are they for permanent display areas?

5. Storage area required.

6. Flexibility required - do you want to use the boards for other purposes eg, exhibition stands, literature displays, even kiosks. Some systems allow for much greater flexibility than others.

7. Set-up and take-down times.

8. Lighting or other electrical supplies required.

9. Method of fixing to board. For example, some units now have fabric 'loop' systems which, using adhesive nylon 'hook' tapes, give considerable flexibility and ease in fixing.

The systems most commonly held by university locations (indeed, the only ones mentioned by name by respondents) are those available from Marler-Haley Ltd. This company can supply a considerable variety of display systems. Pages   and   give, as examples, a selection of panel sizes and 1984 prices for various items. Some are sold in kits, and to give some idea of how items add up, a relatively modest pack giving a display area of just over 50 square feet would cost £240 and weigh 46 lb. Thus, the purchase of such boards will not be undertaken lightly.

Another major supplier of this type of display system is Kepac Ltd. The addresses of both organizations, and that of Photobition, are given below:

Marler-Haley ExpoSystems Ltd, Exposystems House, Queens Road, Barnet, Hertfordshire EN5 4DW; UK: Tel: 01-441-1441.

Kepac Ltd, 25 Ashley Road/60 Oakfield Road, Altrincham, Cheshire, WA15 8EN, UK; Tel: 061-941-1027.

Photobition, 25 Carnwath Road, London SW6, UK; Tel: 01-736-1331.

Lightweight Multiscreen Mk2

Frame and Panel Dimensions

Ladder Frames

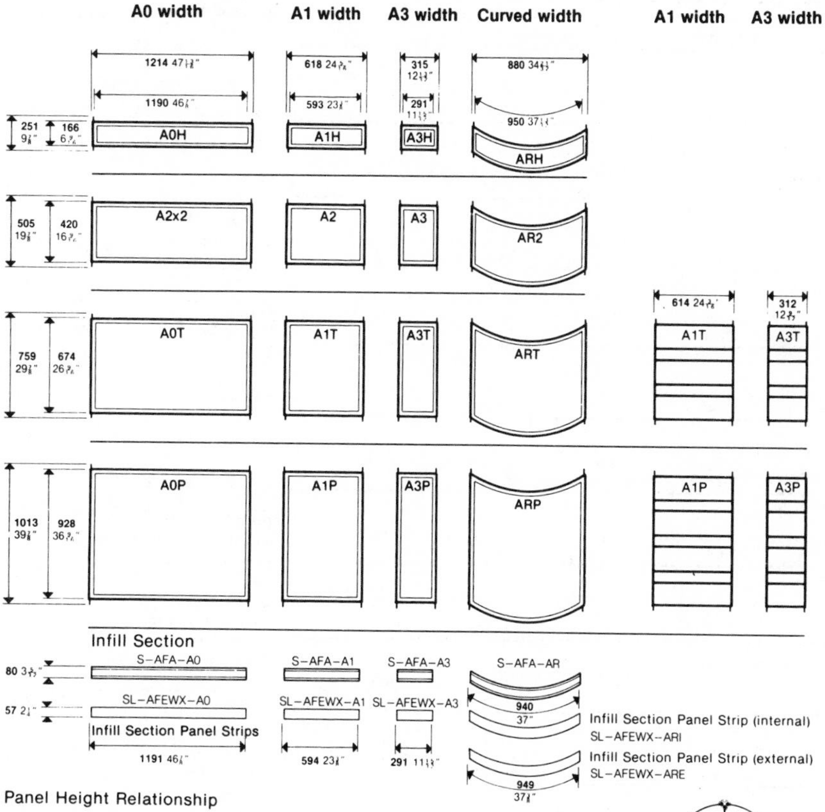

A0 width	A1 width	A3 width	Curved width	A1 width	A3 width

Row 1 (Header panels):
- 1214 47¼" / 1190 46¼" — AOH
- 251 9¼" / 166 6⅝" (height)
- 618 24⅜" / 593 23¼" — A1H
- 315 12⅜" / 291 11⅜" — A3H
- 880 34¾" / 950 37¼" — ARH

Row 2:
- 505 19¾" / 420 16⅜" (height)
- A2x2, A2, A3, AR2

Row 3:
- 759 29⅞" / 674 26⅝" (height)
- A0T, A1T, A3T, ART
- 614 24⅛" — A1T
- 312 12⅜" — A3T

Row 4:
- 1013 39⅞" / 928 36⅝" (height)
- A0P, A1P, A3P, ARP
- A1P, A3P

Infill Section

- 80 3⅛"
- 57 2¼"
- S–AFA–A0
- SL–AFEWX–A0
- S–AFA–A1, S–AFA–A3, S–AFA–AR
- SL–AFEWX–A1, SL–AFEWX–A3
- Infill Section Panel Strips
- 940 37"
- 1191 46¼", 594 23¼", 291 11⅜"
- 949 37¼"
- Infill Section Panel Strip (internal) SL–AFEWX–ARI
- Infill Section Panel Strip (external) SL–AFEWX–ARE

Panel Height Relationship

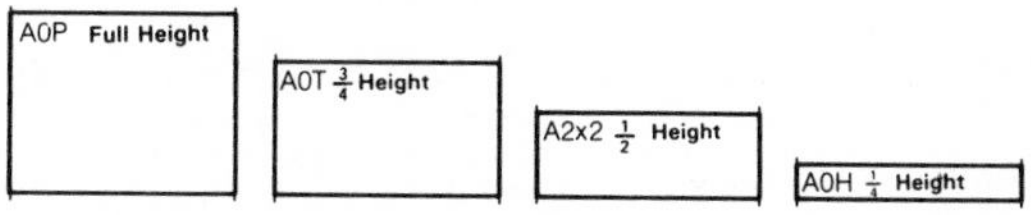

- A0P Full Height
- A0T ¾ Height
- A2x2 ½ Height
- A0H ¼ Height

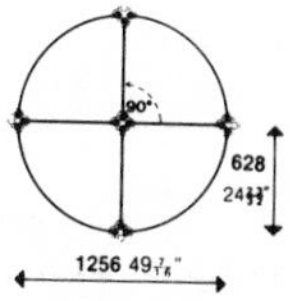

Useful combinations of frame/panel sizes can be chosen to meet a variety
of eye-levels and to support shelving that will provide displays,
demonstration surfaces, desks
and seating at convenient heights.

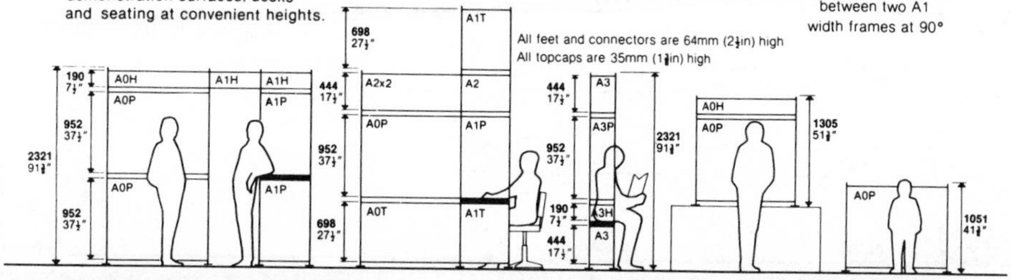

Curved frame radius
The curve is the arc drawn
between two A1
width frames at 90°

- 628 24¾"
- 1256 49⅜"
- 90°

All feet and connectors are 64mm (2½in) high
All topcaps are 35mm (1⅜in) high

Elevation dimensions:
- 190 7½", 952 37½", 2321 91¼", 952 37½"
- 698 27½", 444 17½", 952 37½", 698 27½"
- 444 17½", 952 37½", 190 7½", 444 17½"
- 2321 91¼"
- 1305 51⅜"
- 1051 41⅜"

Frame labels in elevation: A0H, A1H, A1H, A1T, A2x2, A2, A3, A0P, A1P, A1P, A0P, A1P, A3P, A0H, A0P, A0T, A1T, A3H, A3, A0P

Plain Whitex panels — references and prices

Complete Assembly references and prices under this heading include the lightweight frame, panel and a set of clipstrip all assembled ready for immediate use.

	Complete Assembly	Frames	Panels	Clipstrip Sets (4 pieces)
A0H	SL–XX–A0H £14.05	SL–C–A0H £9.10	SL–WX–A0H £3.40	S–Z–A0H £1.55
A2x2	SL–XX–A2x2 £18.40	SL–C–A2x2 £10.20	SL–WX–A2x2 £6.35	S–Z–A2x2 £1.85
A0T	SL–XX–A0T £23.05	SL–C–A0T £11.35	SL–WX–A0T £9.60	S–Z–A0T £2.10
A0P	SL–XX–A0P £27.00	SL–C–A0P £12.55	SL–WX–A0P £12.05	S–Z–A0P £2.40
A1H	SL–XX–A1H £10.45	SL–C–A1H £7.20	SL–WX–A1H £2.30	S–Z–A1H £0.95
A2	SL–XX–A2 £13.00	SL–C–A2 £8.00	SL–WX–A2 £3.75	S–Z–A2 £1.25
A1T	SL–XX–A1T £15.65	SL–C–A1T £8.85	SL–WX–A1T £5.35	S–Z–A1T £1.45
A1P	SL–XX–A1P £18.25	SL–C–A1P £9.75	SL–WX–A1P £6.75	S–Z–A1P £1.75
A3H	SL–XX–A3H £8.40	SL–C–A3H £6.10	SL–WX–A3H £1.65	S–Z–A3H £0.65
A3	SL–XX–A3 £10.30	SL–C–A3 £6.90	SL–WX–A3 £2.50	S–Z–A3 £0.90
A3T	SL–XX–A3T £12.35	SL–C–A3T £7.75	SL–WX–A3T £3.40	S–Z–A3T £1.20
A3P	SL–XX–A3P £14.20	SL–C–A3P £8.65	SL–WX–A3P £4.10	S–Z–A3P £1.45
ARH	SL–XX–ARH £15.20	SL–C–ARH £10.95	SL–WX–ARH £2.80	S–Z–ARH £1.45
AR2	SL–XX–AR2 £19.35	SL–C–AR2 £12.15	SL–WX–AR2 £5.45	S–Z–AR2 £1.75
ART	SL–XX–ART £23.30	SL–C–ART £13.40	SL–WX–ART £7.90	S–Z–ART £2.00
ARP	SL–XX–ARP £27.30	SL–C–ARP £14.70	SL–WX–ARP £10.35	S–Z–ARP £2.25

If required Whitex panels are available covered with Expoloop on one side. Please ask our Sales Department for details.

Adjustable Footpads — Packs of five
S–W–5x5 £5.95

Tubular Connectors — Packs of five
Single — S–W–1x5 £1.20
Two-way — S–W–2x5 £1.80
Three-way — S–W–3x5 £2.40
Four way — S–W–4x5 £2.75

Plastic Top Caps — Packs of five
Single — S–TB–1x5 £0.55
Two-way — S–TB–2x5 £0.60
Three-way — S–TB–3x5 £0.75
Four-way — S–TB–4x5 £0.85

Infill Sections and Panel Strips for Infill Sections

A0 Infill Section — S–AFA–A0 £4.95

A0 Infill Panel Strip
Single-sided Expoloop covered Whitex — SL–AFEWX–A0 £2.10
Plain Whitex — SL–AFWX–A0 £1.10

A1 Infill Section — S–AFA–A1 £3.05

A1 Infill Panel Strip
Single-sided Expoloop covered Whitex — SL–AFEWX–A1 £1.60
Plain Whitex — SL–AFWX–A1 £0.70

A3 Infill Section — S–AFA–A3 £1.95

A3 Infill Panel Strip
Single-sided Expoloop covered Whitex — SL–AFEWX–A3 £1.20
Plain Whitex — SL–AFWX–A3 £0.50

AR Curved Infill Section — S–AFA–AR £7.20

External and Internal Panel strips for curved Infill Section

External
Single-sided Expoloop covered Whitex — SL–AFEWX–ARE £1.95
Plain Whitex — SL–AFWX–ARE £1.00

Internal
Single-sided Expoloop covered Whitex — SL–AFEWX–ARI £1.95
Plain Whitex — SL–AFWX–ARI £1.00

4 PUBLICATION

In this section, we will not advise exactly what to do about publication, but will point out what sort of decisions have to be made.

Nearly all poster sessions form part of a conference which also has conventional, oral presentations. Thus it is quite likely that the issue of publication of poster session 'proceedings' will be linked with that of publication of the conventional proceedings. The publication of conventional proceedings itself can be quite a complex issue and is outside the scope of this guide, except to make a few points relevant to poster sessions:

1. it may seem surprising, but the majority of conferences do not have published proceedings;

2. for those that *do*, the decision to publish is sometimes taken only *after* the conference ("That was a good conference - we should try to publish the proceedings"), or after it is organized but before it actually takes place; and

3. even where a prior decision is taken, often insufficient attention is given to the rights of, and communication with, authors (eg it is not uncommon for someone to be appointed as editor of a proceedings, and for that person to conduct negotiations with a publisher, sign contracts etc, without contacting authors with regard to copyright issues).

Of course, there may be merit in the argument that it is well to see whether a conference merits publication before embarking on it, but there are several points against this approach. It causes publication delay and increases the difficulty of cooperating and communicating with authors. It may also mean that written material and artwork have to be reworked.

Ideally, organizers should decide what they want to do well in advance of the conference. If this involves approaching external publishers, such action should be taken at a very early stage, for no one may want to publish the proceedings and costly preparation would then have been wasted.

The above advice also applies to poster sessions. Having decided on the status of a poster session (eg whether poster presentations are to be treated as equivalent to oral presentations - see earlier sections), organizers then have to decide whether, and how, they are to be published. Are they to ask for conventional hard-copy papers on which the posters will be based? Are these to be refereed? Do they need a clear indication from the author of what will be in the poster presentation, especially if it differs from the written copy? All such questions have to be addressed.

At many conferences, the offer of a paper or a poster may be judged on the basis of a title and abstract alone. In such circumstances the organizers should consider in what form they want a manuscript for publication. If they plan to publish only titles and abstracts of posters, they should clearly say so. The published proceedings should state clearly that it includes no full-papers of posters (this may save many hours of a poor librarian's time!).

Publication considerations will also depend on how the papers are called for and how those for poster treatment are selected. For example, if papers are accepted and *then* it is decided to have some presented as posters and others as conventional papers, contributions presenting posters will be understandably hurt if they find their papers being discriminated against when it comes to publication - especially if the selection for poster presentation was not on grounds of quality, but simply because it was felt more appropriate for the type of material.

The decision on whether to produce/publish abstracts of posters prior to the conference is similar to that for conventional papers. If abstracts are published, they should be arranged so that they tie in with the layout of the presentations in the halls and any guide to the layout.

One further point - whether or not full papers will be published from poster presentations - organizers may want to consider proscribing the literal posting of a written or typed paper at a poster session. Rarely will a manuscript prepared for publication be suitable, without considerable changes, for display on a poster.

Let us assume that the organizers wish to publish the poster papers in some agreed form. They should communicate their decision to contributors or potential contributors as soon as possible. It is important to remember that, in most cases, the contributors will retain copyright in their work unless they explicitly assign it in writing. If the organizers wish to acquire this copyright they should get such assignments from the contributors.

Of course, some may claim that a poster presentation, by itself, constitutes a publication. However, this is a moot point. In a controversial television debate, a scientist (under attack for allegedly stating results on the programme without their being published in the journals) held that he had 'published' the material by reporting the results at a conference. Copyright is another difficult area. To quote from a recent manual on the financial and legal aspects of publishing[4] "Copyright only exists from the point when the material is reduced to writing, drawing or some other permanent form. Reproductions which derive from that written form require permission or else they will be infringing copyright. The derivation may be indirect: if the text, or detailed notes are prepared for a speech and the speech is copied, that requires permission. Purely extempore statements or performances are not the subject of copyright. Such material as discussions at conferences do not usually require the permission of speakers before they are published: contrast the person who delivers a paper, which will be copyright". Generalizing from this it would appear that at the very least, the poster display itself will be copyright, and, of course, any paper derived from it. Any text based on the oral presentation of the poster speaker *may* also be subject to copyright. All this should not present many difficulties to the organizers. The best advice is quite simple - if you wish to publish, make sure to have the copyright holder's permission; if you want copyright, make sure to have it assigned in writing by the copyright holder.

Visitors to a poster session also should not ignore these issues. Kodak Ltd, in a special pamphlet on poster sessions[5], recommend the use of a camera (with Kodak film, naturally) for recording interesting presentations. We would recommend that you at least get the presenters' permission before the clicking the shutter.

5 EVALUATION

In the early days of poster sessions, some organizers attempted to evaluate the usefulness of the sessions. This is probably a worthwhile exercise in a field where poster sessions have not been tried before, and particularly where the conference is one of a series (annual, biannual) where lessons learned can be used in the future. The most systematic method is by questionnaire. Analysing questionnaires can be a laborious business, so it would probably be best to keep them as simple as possible, with different questionnaires for presenters and for other participants. Sample questions would be:

To Participants

1. Did you have sufficient time to see the posters which interested you? YES/NO

2. In your opinion, what percentage of the posters were adequate in design and layout? 0-20 20-40 40-60 60-80 80-100

3. Overall, were the sessions a success? or, Should there be poster sessions at the next ... conference? YES/NO

4. Any suggestions or comments

To Presenters

1. Did you have sufficient time for presenting your poster at the session? YES/NO

2. Did you have sufficient time for setting up? YES/NO

3. Overall, do you think the poster session was a success? or Should we have poster sessions at the next ... conference? YES/NO

4. Any suggestions

The above questions are just examples of the sort of thing that could be used to provide some useful information for future planning. Clearly, organizers could work out what is most appropriate for their needs.

Another technique, useful for presentation to those who do not attend the conference, is to take some photographs of the sessions at regular intervals (as we have said, photographs of particular stands would need the presenters' permission) so that a better idea can be given of relative areas of congestion, overall attendance, etc. A less ostentatious procedure is simply to do counts of the number of people at stands at regular intervals. At one conference I attended, with large booths in the configuration of (ii) and (iii) of Figure 7, the number of people at booths varied from none to eight, with an average of four. It becomes clear, also, when wandering around a poster session, without a specific interest in the subject matter of the posters, that it is not really enough to leave matters of design and presentation entirely to the common sense of the presenters.

6 SUMMARY OF POINTS TO CONSIDER

Below, we summarise the main points that organisers need to consider in running a poster session. This is not intended to be a list so daunting that no one would think of undertaking one, but, rather, it could be used as a useful check list to give some confidence to those who are worried that they have forgotten something of major importance.

1.   Status of Posters
There may be a need to guard against an "inferior" status of posters. Possibilities include:

1.1   acceptance of contributions based on content - method of presentation (oral or poster), to be decided later. Inform presenters of basis for decision.

1.2   positive discrimination - pick some of the best papers for posters.

1.3   treat equally with oral contributions as far as subsequent publication is concerned.

2.   Location of Session

2.1   Suitable sites may include: rooms; small or large halls; hallways and corridors; split sites; near exhibition. All have advantages and disadvantages.

2.2   A layout should be drawn of poster area with poster boards/booths in place in possible configurations. Allot numbers to places.

2.3   Layout and key to posters should be included in conference leaflet or programme for all participants.

2.4   Arrange for direction signs, arrows, etc to poster session area.

3.   Liaison With Presenters On Session

3.1   If possible, nominate organizer for responsibility for posters at the conference. Provide them with a distinctive (eg different colour) badge.

3.2 Prepare distinctive badges for presenters.

3.3 Inform presenters, well in advance of session, of: their own number, place, time and the duration of the session, set-up and dismantling time.

3.4 Inform presenters of: poster board area and configuration; method/s of mounting; need for numbering or titling; hints on design; availability of facilities, like electrical supply, lights, etc.

3.5 Inform presenters of: any prohibitions eg no smoking, no literal posting of typed papers, no selling equipment or publications, overall objective of session (if session is an innovation in the subject field).

4. Poster Boards And Equipment

This is perhaps best treated as a list of questions which organizers should ask.

4.1 Are poster boards and equipment available at the host institution? What type are they? What is the charge, if any, for their use?

4.2 When hiring from an outside organization, ask the questions in 4.1. Also is there a transportation charge?

4.3 For 4.1 and 4.2, is labour available for setting up and dismantling the boards? Who is responsible for seeing that it is done? What charge, if any?

4.4 What other equipment is available or desirable? eg chairs, tables, lights, other electrical supply, pens, pins, stationery. Whose responsibility will it be to see to their provision and maintenance?

4.5 Is there a responsibility on the organizers to provide the numbers and title cards for each poster?

5. Design

5.1 Beyond hints and guidelines of good practice, we recommend the placing of few restraints on presenters.

5.2 Presenters should place particular emphasis on lettering and lines of adequate size and clarity. Recommend a minimum size for titles and text. Suggest also a minimum size for titles and text. Suggest also a minimum line thickness.

5.3   Poster illustrations and text should be in a sequence which is clear to follow. The sequence can if necessary be indicated by numbers or arrows.

5.4   Diagrams and illustrations need clear captions, and an indication of scale in most cases.

6.   Publication

An early decision needs to be made on whether to publish proceedings. If external publishers are to be involved, early liaison (well in advance of the conference) is recommended. As far as poster presentations are concerned, the following points should be particularly taken into account.

6.1   Decide whether to include poster presentations. If so, in what form, eg title and abstract or full paper.

6.2   Will there be refereeing of contributions? Will this differ for poster submissions from that for conventional papers?

6.3   Inform presenters of publication plans, not later than time of call for papers, if possible.

6.4   Obtain requisite permissions or copyright assignments from authors/presenters.

6.5   If poster papers are to be published in full, attempt to establish requirements for diagrams and other graphics for publication, and inform presenters prior to poster preparation.

7.   Evaluation

7.1   Decide whether an evaluation of the poster session is desirable, and if so, how you will go about it.

7.2   If questionnaires are to be used, ensure that some organizer takes responsibility for their construction, administration, collection, analysis and report. Ideally, a draft questionnaire should also be examined by someone other than the designer, to look for ambiguous points or those lacking in clarity.

7.3   Photographs. Ensure that a reasonably clear brief is given to the photographer. Ensure that permissions are obtained before taking photographs of individual presentations.

8. Safety

8.1   Consult host organization for rules on placement of posters, particularly if it is planned to place them in "traffic" areas. Consult them also if you are concerned about their coverage for any potential accident, eg collapsing boards, electrical equipment problems, etc.

REFERENCES

1. *Presentation of Data in Science* L Reynolds; D Simmonds. Martimus Mijhoff. The Hague. 1980-2.

2. *Planning and Producing Audiovisual Materials.* 3rd Edition. J E Kemp; T Y Crowell, New York, 1975.

(Quoted in *Preparing Poster Talks.* A J MacGregor. IEEE Transactions on professional communication. Vol. PC-21 (3), Sept 1978, p 103-5.)

3. *Report on a Poster Session held by the Institute of Information Scientists* submitted to the British Library by C Oppenheim, 1978.

4. *Financial and Legal Aspects*, Scholarly Publishers Guide, J Collins (Ed) Primary Communications Research Centre, 1979.

5. *Communicating through Poster Sessions* P-319 Eastman Kodak Company, 1978.

Further Reading

How, when, why to run poster sessions. C Goldstein *Successful Meetings* August 1976, p 48-50, 74, 77.